THE DEPARTMENT OF HOMELAND SECURITY

Rescue and Prevention: Defending Our Nation

RESCUE AND PREVENTION: Defending Our Nation

THE DEPARTMENT OF HOMELAND SECURITY

MICHAEL KERRIGAN

MASON CREST PUBLISHERS
www.masoncrest.com

Mason Crest Publishers Inc.
370 Reed Road
Broomall, PA 19008
(866) MCP-BOOK (toll free)
www.masoncrest.com

First printing

1 2 3 4 5 6 7 8 9 10

Library of Congress Cataloging-in-Publication Data on file
at the Library of Congress

ISBN 1-59084-409-2

Editorial and design by
Amber Books Ltd.
Bradley's Close
74–77 White Lion Street
London N1 9PF
www.amberbooks.co.uk

Project Editor: Michael Spilling
Design: Graham Curd
Picture Research: Natasha Jones

Printed and bound in Jordan

Picture credits
Corbis: 6; Federal Emergency Management Agency: 30, 62; Popperfoto: 32, 67, 68, 70, 73, 78; Topham Picturepoint: 8, 11, 13, 17, 18, 20, 22, 25, 26, 29, 31, 35, 36, 37, 39, 40, 42, 44, 47, 48, 49, 51, 54, 56, 57, 59, 60, 64, 69, 77, 79, 80, 83, 84; TRH: 14; U.S. Department of Defense: 43, 52, 74, 87, 88, 89.
Front cover: Topham Picturepoint, Popperfoto (bottom left).

DEDICATION

This book is dedicated to those who perished in the terrorist attacks of September 11, 2001, and to all the committed individuals who continually serve to defend freedom and protect the American people.

CONTENTS

INTRODUCTION

September 11, 2001, saw terrorism cast its lethal shadow across the globe. The deaths inflicted at the Twin Towers, at the Pentagon, and in Pennsylvania were truly an attack on the world and civilization itself. However, even as the impact echoed around the world, the forces of decency were fighting back: Americans drew inspiration from a new breed of previously unsung, everyday heroes. Amid the smoking rubble, firefighters, police officers, search-and-rescue, and other "first responders" made history. The sacrifices made that day will never be forgotten.

Out of the horror and destruction, we have fought back on every front. When the terrorists struck, their target was not just the United States, but also the values that the American people share with others all over the world who cherish freedom. Country by country, region by region, state by state, we have strengthened our public-safety efforts to make it much more difficult for terrorists.

Others have come to the forefront: from the Coast Guard to the Border Patrol, a wide range of agencies work day and night for our protection. Before the terrorist attacks of September 11, 2001, launched them into the spotlight, the courage of these guardians went largely unrecognized, although in truth, the sense of service was always honor enough for them. We can never repay the debt we owe them, but by increasing our understanding of the work they do, the *Rescue and Prevention: Defending Our Nation* books will enable us to better appreciate our brave defenders.

Steven L. Labov—CISM, MSO, CERT 3

Chief of Department, United States Search and Rescue Task Force

Left: Armed and alert, a National Guardsman stands ready to defend his homeland at a moment's notice.

THE CHALLENGE

Officially, the 21st century began on January 1, 2001, but in hindsight, the months that followed seemed an interlude falling outside of time. The century was nine months old when, out of the blue sky of a bright fall morning, terror came rushing from the sky to announce that a new historical era had begun.

The hideous symbolism of the outrage of September 11, 2001, was unmistakable: the twin towers of the World Trade Center were recognizable the world over as an image of the economic energy and enterprise of the United States. The Pentagon, in Washington, D.C., was, and remains, the headquarters of the armed forces of the greatest military power the world has ever seen. There was nothing symbolic, however, about the thousands of innocent lives lost, the countless others injured, the grief of their families, or the pain of the United States as a whole.

The terrorist fanatics of Al Qaeda had hurled down a bloody challenge to the world's greatest democracy. Would it now collapse like a stricken skyscraper, or stand firm for freedom and justice? The global superpower had suddenly become vulnerable. How was it now to protect itself against an

Left: A scene from "Ground Zero," October 2001, as workers sort through the still-smoking rubble of the World Trade Center, a hideous testimony to fanaticism, hatred, and cruel terror.

enemy who followed none of the old rules?

President George W. Bush believed that the United States did have the resources and courage to fight back against terror. He recognized, however, that the struggle would call for new strategies, new attitudes, and new ways of working. With this end in mind, he established the Department of Homeland Security to coordinate the response of the many different agencies responsible for guaranteeing the safety of Americans.

A WORLD POWER

The 20th century ended with the United States acknowledged as the world's unrivaled superpower, its peace and prosperity apparently assured. It is important to remember as we enter what are likely to be difficult and dangerous times, that America has fought for its freedoms—and those of other people around the world—many times before.

The United States was born from conflict when American colonists forcibly broke away from the British. Their freedom was fought for by the first citizen militias, the direct ancestors of our modern National Guard. Subsequently, the new country would have to defend its independence on the field of battle several times in the course of the 19th century. Indeed, it fought wars not only with Britain, but also with France, Mexico, and Spain. Democracy has always had to be defended.

This belief propelled the United States onto the world stage in 1917, intervening to bring an end to the bloody stalemate of World War I. President Woodrow Wilson had, for some time, tried using

Just four days after the Al Qaeda attack, with hopes of finding survivors not yet quite extinguished, rescue workers sift through the wreckage of "Ground Zero."

diplomatic influence to end the carnage of the trenches; when these attempts failed, he felt the country had no alternative but action. The aggressive militarism of the Kaiser's Germany had to be resisted, Americans felt—and they volunteered to fight for the freedom of Europe in the hundreds of thousands.

Within a generation, Germany was on the march again, this time under the ruthless leadership of the dictator Adolf Hitler. With his creed of nationalistic hatred, he succeeded in mobilizing the mass of ordinary Germans, demoralized as they were by the years of economic stagnation and political powerlessness that had followed Germany's defeat in 1918. The Jews, said the leader of the National

AN OFFICE FOR ACTION

From a speech by President George W. Bush, September 20, 2001:

"Our response involves far more than instant retaliation and isolated strikes. Americans should not expect one battle, but a lengthy campaign, unlike any other we have ever seen. It may include dramatic strikes, visible on TV, and covert operations, secret even in success. We will starve terrorists of funding, turn them one against another, drive them from place to place, until there is no refuge or no rest. And we will pursue nations that provide aid or safe haven to terrorism. Every nation, in every region, now has a decision to make. Either you are with us, or you are with the terrorists. From this day forward, any nation that continues to harbor or support terrorism will be regarded by the United States as a hostile regime.

"Our nation has been put on notice: we are not immune from attack. We will take defensive measures against terrorism to protect Americans. Today, dozens of federal departments and agencies, as well as state and local governments, have responsibilities affecting homeland security. These efforts must be coordinated at the highest level. So tonight I announce the creation of a Cabinet-level position reporting directly to me—the Office of Homeland Security."

Right: Regarded with some disdain when he came to office on the grounds of his youth and inexperience, President Bush has won worldwide respect by his resolute handling of the War Against Terror.

U.S. President Woodrow Wilson and General John J. Pershing review troops in France in 1919 after the victorious conclusion of the First World War. Many had opposed U.S. involvement as an unnecessary entanglement in other people's problems, yet it marked the beginning of America's emergence as a world power.

Socialist (Nazi) Party, were the great sickness in German society, the source of all the country's many woes. Without the Jews, he promised, Germany would be able to assume her rightful place in the world: **anti-Semitism** became the great cause around which Germans rallied.

With its contempt for the idea of debate or disagreement and for the legal niceties of the electoral process, **fascism** was a political system that was the exact opposite of democratic. Yet, along with other fascist strongmen—most famously Benito Mussolini in Italy—Hitler did seem to be speaking for the "little guy" in the street. Hence, the huge tide of popular support, which bore Germany and Italy along as they set out to bring the whole of Europe under their control.

On the other side of the world, meanwhile, military rulers in Japan were determined to extend their country's rule throughout the Pacific region—their alliance with fascist Europe was the original "axis of evil." As Hitler's henchmen set in motion their final solution to the "Jewish problem," Japanese forces were massacring men, women, and children in China and Korea.

Again, the United States sought at first to find a way to peace through quiet intervention behind the scenes. However, the attack on Pearl Harbor on December 7, 1941, made such detachment impossible. Forced to fight for freedom in the world, the United States did not shirk the task. Indeed, many feel that the nation came of age in the four-year struggle that ensued.

THE COLD WAR

The United States emerged from World War II in 1945 as a superpower. So, too, however, did another nation of a different kind: the Union of Soviet Socialist Republics, or USSR.

In 1917, Russian revolutionaries had overthrown the oppressive rule of the old emperors, or czars, only to establish an even more ferocious tyranny in its place—**Communism**. Murdering their political opponents, or dispatching them to die in distant labor camps, the Communists took an iron grip on every area of Soviet life. Businessmen and entrepreneurs (even hard-working peasants) were accused of exploiting their workers and branded "class enemies," becoming the social scapegoats that the Jews had been for Nazi Germany.

The longer-term effects of this policy would eventually prove catastrophic—without men and women of initiative and energy, the USSR was economically doomed. However, in the immediate term, it created cohesion and a sense of social purpose. Hitler's invasion of Russia in 1941 and the bitter fighting of the "Great Patriotic War" that followed brought the whole country into line behind its leader, Joseph Stalin. His final victory in that fearful conflict lent his rule an air of legitimacy in the eyes of many Soviets, assuring the survival of a regime combining monstrous evil with the most abject economic incompetence.

Having thrown back the German invaders from their territories, Stalin's forces proceeded to "liberate" the German-occupied states of Eastern Europe, turning Poland, Czechoslovakia, Hungary, Romania, and the eastern half of Germany into Communist states. Only the presence of American and British armies prevented the wholesale **annexation** of Germany.

In the years that followed, the Soviet Union cemented its hold behind what British statesman Winston Churchill called the "Iron Curtain." The United States was forced into an ever-escalating **arms** race to protect itself and its democratic allies against the Communist threat. This uncomfortable confrontation between East and West, known as the **Cold War**, stopped short of all-out conflict

Vladimir Ilyich Ulyanov, better known as "Lenin" (1870–1924), stern father of the Russian Revolution, glowers down from a Soviet-era public building. Although not quite the murderous monster his successor Stalin was, Lenin was ruthless in his contempt for democratic freedoms: no individual could be allowed to impede the march of Communism.

between the superpowers, but a number of "proxy wars" were fought in various third-world countries. In the Korean War (1950–1953) and in the Vietnam War (1964–1974), U.S. forces were compelled to take action on the ground to defend democratic

"Courage," says the sign outside this Guildford, England, pub, blown up by an IRA bomb in 1974. It was not an exhortation to firmness, as it happens, merely a mark that the bar was owned by the Courage brewery—but the British experience did prove that public resolve could prevail over terror in the longer term.

nations against invasion by satellite states of the Soviet Union.

In time, however, the costs of the arms race proved too much for a Communist "command economy," in which bureaucratic organization proved no substitute for the entrepreneurial spirit that had

LIVING WITH TERROR

The threat of terrorism has been one of the realities of European life for many years. The troubles of Northern Ireland have often spilled over onto the streets of mainland Britain. Terrorists representing the Irish Republican Army (IRA) have attacked targets ranging from British Army recruiting offices to train stations, shopping malls, office buildings, tourist sites, and crowded bars in London and in other cities.

There have been similar problems in Spain, where members of the separatist group ETA have been trying to bomb and assassinate their way to independence for the northerly Basque country. (ETA stands for Euskadi Ta Askatasuna, which means "Basque Homeland and Freedom.")

Whatever the levels of "soft" support for national causes, in neither Northern Ireland nor the Basque country can the terrorists claim to be acting for the people as a whole. Nor can they claim to have succeeded in intimidating the populations they have attacked over a period of decades. For the most part, civilian populations have learned to live with the dangers posed by terrorist extremists. And any political advances that have been made, have been made by discussion and debate.

made the U.S. economy so strong. The Soviets' invasion of Afghanistan in 1979 to prop up a "puppet" government under pressure was to prove one expansionist measure too many. With its forces mired in an unwinnable war and its ramshackle economy

In the "people's democracies" of Eastern Europe, people were free only to do as they were told: any genuinely democratic aspirations they might have got short shrift from their Soviet overlords. Risings against Communist rule were put down ruthlessly by military force—most notoriously in Prague, the Czechoslovakian capital, in 1968.

straining to cope, the USSR was brought slowly but surely to its knees in the decade that followed.

AMERICAN ASCENDANCY

The demolition of the Berlin Wall by cheering crowds in November 1989 was the emblematic moment in the fall of Communism. For almost 30 years this structure separated East Berliners from their fellow citizens and relatives in the West. American culture, as popularly exemplified by cartoon characters and burger bars, was now recognized and sought after the whole world over. For years, McDonald's, Mickey Mouse, and Michael Jackson had represented the Western lifestyle so many people had been denied, but to which they had, at the same time, always secretly aspired.

Yet even amid the euphoria and the globalization of U.S. culture, there were signs that peace was under threat. One of the newly liberated countries, Yugoslavia, was an unhappy confederation of long-standing antagonistic nations in the Balkan region of southeastern Europe. Held together only by Communist force, Yugoslavia responded to its new freedom by spiraling into bitter conflict. Elsewhere, there were reminders that Communism might not be the only threat to freedom and peace when Saddam Hussein's Iraqi forces invaded Kuwait at the end of 1990.

As we have seen, however, the United States had learned the hard way of the need to arm itself for peace. Through the tense decades of the Cold War, it had developed the capacity to bring overwhelming force to bear on any state that sought to upset the international order. Serbia, bent on conquest in the Balkans, was to discover this to her cost; as indeed was Saddam Hussein in the Gulf War of 1991.

NEW REALITIES

But states were no longer the only organizations to be acting on the world stage. International terrorism was on the rise since the 1960s. The most notorious incidents of this kind were the "skyjackings" conducted by Palestinians protesting Israeli occupation of their lands. Aimed at bringing their **grievances** to the attention of the

world, the hijacking of civilian airliners tested to the very limits the notion that "any publicity is good publicity"—and, in time, the practice was abandoned by the Palestinians.

The methods of terrorism were, however, eagerly embraced by another generation of even more fanatical fighters as a new wave of Islamic fundamentalism swept across the Middle East. Where earlier generations of Arabs were motivated by a mood of nationalism—a desire to be independent from the domination of the rich and powerful countries of the West—the fundamentalists spurn what they regard as ungodly and inglorious half-measures. For them, nothing is more important than Islam. Indeed, they draw inspiration from a literal-minded interpretation of the thoughts of the Prophet Muhammad as recorded in the Koran, and seek to sweep away all signs of modernity and Westernization—including the state of Israel—from the Middle East. As many scholars have pointed out, Islamic fundamentalism may be expressed as religious fervor, but many Muslims feel a more worldly resentment toward an affluent Western consumer culture from which they feel excluded.

Although fundamentalist groups like Al Qaeda may work with "**rogue states**" in the furtherance of their cause, they scorn the

Left: Thrown up by the Communist rulers of East Berlin who feared their citizens' mass-defection to the Western sector, the Berlin Wall stood as a symbol of oppression through three decades. Its demolition by demonstrators in 1989 came as a joyous confirmation for the world that, after years of mounting crisis, Soviet-style Communism had finally collapsed.

artificial boundaries appointed by politics. Their identity is intrinsically transnational, owing no allegiance to any one government, while their membership may be drawn from Muslim communities across the Islamic world. This makes them a peculiarly elusive enemy. For the very reason that they cannot command the organizational resources of the centralized state, they do not have the sort of well-defined structure that can easily be identified and then destroyed. Al Qaeda, for instance, is believed to operate in over 40 countries and to be so loosely constituted that the destruction of one cell would have little impact on the organization as a whole.

ENEMIES WITHIN

It is worth remembering that terrorism is not just a threat from outside. On April 19, 1995, a huge truck bomb blew away the entire front of Oklahoma City's Murrah Building—and destroyed America's peace of mind. This attack cost the lives of 168 men, women, and children, and another 500 were injured, many quite seriously. It was, at this point, the most serious terrorist attack on U.S. soil—and it was the work not of foreign terrorists, but of self-styled "patriots."

Right: Presenting a very different picture from the force that had terrorized the tiny kingdom of Kuwait, defeated Iraqi prisoners are marched to captivity in Saudi Arabia at the end of the 1991 Gulf War. Despite his defeat, however, dictator Saddam Hussein would remain in power in Iraq, sidestepping the sanctions of the international community to rebuild his war machine.

WHO IS OSAMA BIN LADEN?

Described as "modest, almost shy," Osama bin Laden was born in Saudi Arabia to a family that came originally from nearby Yemen. Thanks to his family's construction fortune, bin Laden was born to great wealth and privilege.

He went to Afghanistan to help his Muslim brothers in the Mujahideen against the Soviet invaders. By all accounts, he was a courageous **guerrilla** fighter. Yet to bin Laden's fundamentalist way of thinking, there is no difference between Soviet Communists and American democrats: indeed, both are infidels, godless enemies of Allah. Al Qaeda, the organization he leads, has been blamed for the 1998 bombings in Nairobi, Kenya, and Dar es Salaam, Tanzania, and for the 2000 bombing of the USS *Cole* in Yemen.

Bin Laden has given few interviews and has been reluctant to acknowledge responsibility for particular acts. But his attitude is chillingly clear from his casual comments regarding the bombers who killed six U.S. soldiers at their base in Riyadh, Saudi Arabia, in 1995: "We look at these young men as great heroes and martyrs who followed the steps of the prophet, peace be upon him. We called and they answered."

Left: The face of the world's most wanted man gives away little about the inward character of the individual believed to have given the order for the attacks of September 11, 2001. A fanatical fighter for Islam, Osama bin Laden's life has been dedicated to the destruction of the West.

Americans were shaken to learn that some individuals consider the federal government of the United States to be the enemy. For Timothy McVeigh, a white supremacist and one of the men responsible for the bombing, the government is an alien "occupying force." The government's offense, as far as the white supremacist right is concerned, is to admit immigrants to the country and to promote the welfare of those nonwhite groups already here (including Jews, African Americans, and Hispanics). Rather than protecting white Americans from the encroachments of such groups, the federal government places restrictions on these "patriots'" rights to carry arms. Outlandish as it may sound, the similarities between white and Islamic fundamentalist groups are clear. Both movements rationalize the rage of groups who feel marginalized by the normal political processes of their countries. And, like the racist frenzy of the Nazis, the anger of the white supremacists stems from a profound sense that a people who should be privileged by destiny are, in reality, living impoverished and powerless lives.

NEW RISKS

Used in both the first World Trade Center attack of 1993 and the Oklahoma City blast two years later, bombs are, unfortunately, only the first weapons in the terrorist **armory**. They are also among the least potent. Deadly as their consequences often are, their range is limited and their effects immediate. In recent years, however, a range of more insidious weapons has become available. There are growing fears about the possibility of **cyberterrorism** or the use of chemical or biological weapons. The prospect of **bioterrorism** is peculiarly frightening, since its action is both invisible and delayed, and its effects may be carried far and wide among the population by secondary infection.

Despite the comparatively small number of actual casualties, the anthrax attacks that followed the atrocities of September 11, 2001, were profoundly disturbing—and it makes little difference whether

Veiled Pakistani women, supporters of the Jamat-e-Islam party, protest against Israeli incursions into Palestinian territories in April 2002. For militants across the Muslim world, the demonization of the United States and Israel has enabled a wide range of otherwise mutually hostile factions to unite around a common cause.

Rescue workers and FBI investigators crowd the shattered ruins of Oklahoma City's Murrah Building after the terrible truck bombing of April 19, 1995.

they were the work of a lone screwball or an international terrorist conspiracy. Whoever was behind them, they highlighted the potential for panic and widespread disruption, and the inadequacy of the preventive procedures that were then in place.

Although a minor situation in comparison to the World Trade Center and Pentagon attacks, the anthrax scare still served as a warning to America. The world today is a dangerous place. Our armed forces, although formidable, cannot be expected to guarantee our protection against enemies who may strike by any means.

An oil well blazes out of control after Iraq's invasion of Kuwait in 1990: Saddam's actions represented not only a human, but also an economic and environmental calamity for the Middle East.

THE RESPONSE

There is no denying the fact that the outrages of September 11, 2001, took the United States by surprise—and hit the world's most powerful nation where it hurt. Americans reeled from the shock, profoundly perplexed. What had caused this? And what was to be the response?

Defenseless and innocent civilians found themselves on a front-line of someone else's making. In a matter of hours, and on a scale never before seen, thousands had died. The nation was eager to strike back, but unsure where the blow should fall. Such frustration could easily have led to demoralization and paranoia. True, the valor of the rescue services was inspirational, but there was a real danger that Americans might lose their nerve at this crucial moment. The greatest military machine the world has ever seen and its formidable intelligence apparatus had been powerless against a few determined terrorists armed only with simple blades.

Calm courage prevailed. Establishing the Department of Home-land Security, the president acknowledged the gravity of the threat, but at the same time asserted his complete confidence in the nation's

Left: The attacks of September 11, 2001, had one positive consequence, at least: that of reminding Americans just how much they loved their homeland. Sales of the Stars and Stripes soared in stores America-wide: here, a Washington, D.C., Park police officer flies the flag as he goes about his duties.

ability to confront it. An umbrella organization, the office has a role, not to create new capabilities for our defense, but to coordinate the work of existing agencies. The United States already has the material and human resources necessary for its own defense; the task of the new office is to bring them to battle-readiness.

OPERATION NOBLE EAGLE

The scrambling of F-16 fighters in the immediate aftermath of the terrorist attacks was of great symbolic importance. The sight of them patrolling the skies above our major cities was an important show of strength—for the benefit both of the American people and their enemies. These fighters could indeed have prevented a repetition of the World Trade Center or Pentagon attacks, although to shoot down an airliner full of passengers would be, by any standards, a desperate measure.

Of more practical significance, perhaps, was the mobilization of the National Guard to beef up airport security. Again, this sent a message both to America itself and to its enemies in the outside world: the people of the United States are resolved to defend themselves, standing by the cause of freedom as they have done so many times before. The involvement of the National Guard was especially crucial, representing as it did a return to the oldest traditions of the nation. Directly descended from those citizen militias that defended the first European settlers against attack, and which afterward drove the British colonists from these shores, the National Guard is a neighborhood-based force of ordinary Americans who have sworn to defend their home communities. By rallying to the flag at this

An F-16 fighter patrols the skies, armed against just about any eventuality—yet such high-tech weaponry may provide little protection against the desperate terrorist. Faced with an enemy fearless in his fanaticism, we are going to have to find resources of our own, summoning up all our patriotic pride and collective courage.

moment, ordinary Americans proclaimed their readiness to come to the defense of their homeland—and sent a message of symbolic importance that is more profound than the deployment of regular forces would have implied.

Not that our armed forces were idle. The Army, Air Force, Marines, and Navy were soon in action, taking the fight to Al Qaeda in the mountains and cave complexes of Afghanistan. But the smashing of the terrorists and their Taliban protectors on the ground has overshadowed what may, in time, prove to have been

The scene we never dreamt of seeing, outside some absurdly far-fetched action movie: armed National Guardsmen patrolling the streets of downtown New York City. The events of September 11, 2001, have changed America profoundly and perhaps forever: we will have to get used to living in a state of constant high alert.

a far more significant development: the establishment of the Department of Homeland Security under Governor Tom Ridge.

THE MAN OF THE MOMENT

On October 8, 2001, Governor Tom Ridge of Pennsylvania was sworn in as director of the president's new Department of Homeland Security. Ridge has come a long way from his working-class roots in Pittsburgh's Steel Valley. After gaining a scholarship to Harvard in 1967, he interrupted his law studies to serve in Vietnam,

Tom Ridge, Governor of Pennsylvania and George W. Bush's choice to head up his new Office of Homeland Security: the safety of America could be in his hands. Fortunately, his distinguished record of service in the military and in government recommends him.

where he was decorated for valor. Back home in America, politics proved to be a battlefield of a different sort, but Ridge has consistently shown himself to be a tough, yet fair-minded, fighter. At his swearing in, he spelled out the principles he planned to introduce, arguing that what was required was not a new set of skills or capabilities, but the rediscovery and redirection of a spirit that had stood America in good stead throughout its history:

"Americans should find comfort in knowing that millions of their fellow citizens are working every day to ensure our security at every level—federal, state, county, municipal. These are dedicated professionals who are good at what they do. I've seen it up close, as governor of Pennsylvania.

"But there may be gaps in the system. The job of the Department of Homeland Security will be to identify those gaps and work to close them. The size and scope of this challenge are immense. The president's executive order states that we must detect, prepare for, prevent, protect against, respond to, and recover from terrorist attacks, an extraordinary mission. But we will carry it out....

"It's called Homeland Security. While the effort will begin here, it will require the involvement of Americans at every level. Everyone in the homeland must play a part. I ask the American people for their patience, their awareness, and their resolve. This job calls for a national effort. We've seen it before, whether it was building the

Right: A National Guardsman patrols the precincts of Los Angeles International Airport just a few weeks after the September 11, 2001, outrages.

NEEDLES IN HAYSTACKS

Almost 500 million people a year enter America through established border crossings; many thousands more slip across illegally or hop ashore at unobserved landing places. Any one of these visitors could be carrying a weapon of mass destruction, which might be as small as a scent bottle—might, indeed, even be a scent bottle full of biotoxin for aerosol dispersion. Any one of the more than 120 million passenger vehicles that enter the country each year could have a "suitcase bomb" in the trunk: an improvised nuclear device to be feared as a source of radiation rather than for the force of its blast.

However hard we watch our 7,000 miles (11,272 km) of land frontier and our many thousands more of coastline, how are we to apprehend those terrorists—whether foreign or homegrown—already in our midst? The fear could paralyze us if we let it. The answer is to combine vigilance with calm, for these comings and goings are vital to the life of the nation. If we are not to travel or admit visitors or allow the free-flowing importation or distribution of goods, we will effectively be surrendering, doing the work of the terrorists for them.

Left: Whatever defenses we may put up, in the end, a frontier can only be an imaginary line on the ground; here, pedestrians stride from Mexico into the United States. Our prosperity depends on welcoming foreign visitors and the trade they bring, but our safety may depend on our maintaining control of comings and goings.

B-52H bombers over Afghanistan have waged a type of warfare with which America's armed forces have long been familiar. The work of the conventional armed forces remains crucial, yet at the same time, we have all had to recognize that the bitterest battles may have to be fought much nearer home.

transcontinental railroad, fighting World War II, or putting a man on the moon.

"There are some things we can do immediately, and we will. Others will take more time. But we will find something for every American to do. My friends in the Army Corps of Engineers remind me of their motto, 'The difficult, we do immediately. The impossible takes a little longer.'"

A NEW WAY OF THINKING

The establishment of an administrative office may seem absurdly undramatic after the fearful inferno of September 11. Yet the creation of the Department of Homeland Security indicates the president's recognition that what is required in our present situation may not necessarily be ever more, ever "smarter" firepower in the field. While high-tech weaponry has proved its value in Afghanistan and elsewhere, what is needed most immediately is a higher level of preparation and administrative control at home.

Defense Secretary Donald H. Rumsfeld pledges that terrorist fanaticism and ruthlessness will be matched by American resolve as he unveils plans for the offensive known as "Operation Enduring Freedom," September 25, 2001.

We must be aware of the threat of biological attack. This has been a theoretical possibility for a long time now, but has suddenly come to seem all too possible. Consider, for example, a biological attack by aerosol on a city subway. The weapon would be discreet—a perfume bottle or other small spray—and the attack itself might pass entirely unnoticed. The victims themselves, rushing commuters, might easily be unaware that they had been "hit," and several days might pass before they started feeling any ill effects.

A United States Coast Guard cutter stands sentinel beside a vital bridge over the Hudson River, New York. No one knows where, when, or how the terrorists may strike next, so all government agencies have been operating under conditions of ceaseless vigilance.

MANAGING THE FEAR

A psychologist at the U.S. Department of Veterans Affairs Medical Center, New York, Paul Ofman has studied the sort of mental stresses a bioterrorist attack may cause. The great problem is, he says, that with no warning, no loud explosion—indeed, no indication that an attack has taken place at all—individuals have no way of knowing whether or not they have been affected.

"Evidence that the tornado or hurricane has come and gone is pretty unambiguous," he told Scott Sleek of the APA (American Psychological Association) *Monitor*. "But when it's something that contaminates the air you breathe, when people don't really know what's going on, there's much more distress. Where is it? Where did it happen? When will it end? What are the long-term effects? All these questions raise the risk for panic."

Even then, when they saw their doctors, the significance of their symptoms might escape notice. Meanwhile, they would unwittingly be passing on their infections to their families, friends, and fellow workers. In such a situation, we have to rethink what we understand by the word "defense": an alert member of the public who spotted the attack as it happened or a nurse or doctor who was quick to see the signs thereafter would be of more value in such a situation than an aircraft carrier or tank division.

It is not enough for us to be alert. We have to know what we are on the lookout for, and our emergency services have to be thoroughly schooled in the handling of every conceivable sort of emergency. Courage, admirable as it is, is no substitute for expertise; nor can energy and enthusiasm do the work of careful preparation. Some years ago, for example, a collaborative exercise was staged in which police officers, firefighters, and National Guard squads worked side-by-side to tackle a bioterrorist emergency. In an impressively well-oiled exercise, they moved in quickly and efficiently and had the whole area cleared of people and thoroughly washed down in a matter of minutes. This would have been the correct procedure in the aftermath of a chemical attack. In the case of a biological attack, it would have been a calamity, as using water would assist in the dispersal of the biological agent.

Our health care workers must be trained to recognize the early signs of a bioterrorist attack. The first symptoms of a fatal disease may be nothing worse than aching joints and a few sniffles. The sooner such diseases can be identified, the better the chance of successfully treating them—and slowing their spread.

All services, not just medics, must learn to deal with the effects of panic, which can too easily turn a minor incident into a mass tragedy. There is no greater toxin than terror. When terrorists released sarin, a nerve gas, on the Tokyo subway in 1995, no fewer than 5,500 people needed medical treatment. The vast majority,

Right: Any of these riders on the Washington, D.C., Metro could conceivably be armed with a scent-bottle-sized biological weapon— and all could be casualties in the event of a biological or chemical attack. The most disturbing aspect of the new terrorism has been its way of turning everyday things (airliners, the mail) into weapons.

Rescue workers tend to casualties of the 1995 Tokyo subway attack: terrified commuters collapsed in their hundreds, bringing chaos and confusion to the entire city. Only later would it emerge that few had actually been in contact with the sarin gas itself. In an incident like this, panic may be the most potent poison.

however, turned out to have been suffering the effects of shock; only a handful had actually been affected by the gas itself. Law enforcement officers, firefighters, and other services are likely to find their relief efforts hampered by the mass hysteria that often follows incidents of this kind. The public must remember the importance of keeping calm whatever the danger. No one was ever saved by losing his head in a time of peril.

While frontline emergency rescue workers are unlikely to flee screaming from the scene of an atrocity, this does not mean they are immune from the effects of panic. It can be extraordinarily hard to maintain efficient procedures amid a general atmosphere of hysteria, as responders to the 1995 Tokyo subway attack discovered. With panic-stricken people filling stairways and elevators, milling around subway entrances, and collapsing in the roadways outside, rescue workers had great difficulty reaching the site of the attack.

It takes discipline for operational effectiveness to be maintained in such circumstances—for which exercises can provide only partial preparation. Managing panic is among the most important aspects of emergency relief in a situation of this kind. Indeed, in some cases, it is as important as actual decontamination. What rescue services

Cleanup work continues at the Pentagon, Washington D.C., singled out by the Al Qaeda terrorists as headquarters of the U.S. military.

STAYING COOL

If the establishment of an office—all phones and filing cabinets—seems a muted response to the apocalyptic events of September 11, 2001, that (as we have seen) is the whole point. Strip away the drama from acts of terrorism and you can keep the fear in proportion. Then you can come up with a sensibly managed, appropriate response. People are killed and injured in terrorist outrages, but people are killed and injured in other ways every day—this is not a reason for complacency, but it is good grounds for remaining calm. We should never underestimate the evil of terrorism, but neither should we overestimate its power. If we maintain our vigilance and keep our heads, we need not fear.

"Because of September 11," says Quentin Banks of the Maryland Emergency Management Agency (MEMA), "everyone is focused on the terrorism aspect. But a lot of the planning that goes on is the same type of response whether it's bioterrorism or **pandemic** flu."

All hands to the pumps! If September 11, 2001, was an inspiration as well as a tragedy, that is in large part because of the many deeds of individual heroism the catastrophe gave rise to; the number of Americans who went so far "beyond the call of duty." Just one example was that of former fire chief Joseph Curry, who came out of retirement to help organize rescuers at Ground Zero.

need is not the most expensive equipment, but equipment that functions and will not buckle under the strain of a big emergency.

COOPERATION

The effects of public panic might be intensified by organizational difficulties. Confusion is almost inevitable when a number of different services are asked to collaborate under extreme pressure. Hence the need for the Department of Homeland Security, which oversees the work of no fewer than 40 separate agencies. These range

An airman carries out a safety check on a United States Air Force F-16 Fighting Falcon. In the worst case, they could have helped prevent any repetition of the September 11, 2001, attacks, although for the most part their presence was a matter of symbolism.

from the U.S. Congress and its Terrorism and Homeland Security Subcommittee to the Food and Safety Inspectorate; from the CIA to the Park Police; from the Secret Service to the National Disaster Medical System. Each of these bodies has its own traditions, its own "culture," its own attitudes; there may even be competitive tensions and a certain wariness between the organizations.

Yet even when agencies are willing to cooperate, they may have their own—often quite different—ways of doing things. At the scene of a terrorist attack, compare the instincts of a law enforcement agency, like a local police force or the FBI, with those of a rescue service, like a fire department or paramedic crew. For the former, this is a "crime scene," to be protected as much as possible and searched for evidence; for the latter, it is an outbreak to be suppressed and its casualties cleared with all possible urgency.

Professor Loch Johnson of the University of Georgia has described America's antiterrorist establishment as a "bowl of spaghetti"—so many different agencies communicating (or not communicating) along a complicated chain of command. The task of the Department of Homeland Security is to make this bewildering array of organizations function as a single entity, pulling together in a single common cause: the defense and protection of the United States.

Effective Homeland Security is likely to be "homely" security: a matter of doing simple things efficiently. A clear chain of command will be far more important than any amount of high-tech weaponry, while all the intelligence information in the world will not help us if it cannot be communicated readily from one agency to another.

IN THE FRONTLINE

The police officers and firefighters who ran into the wreckage of the World Trade Center to help their fellow New Yorkers were doing what they did every day—their duty. For too long, we have taken such everyday heroism for granted. Now we recognize the dangers of this work and realize that those dangers may increase.

On September 11, 2001, the spotlight fell on the "first responders," those who routinely put their lives on the line. On that day, they risked their lives—and lost. As we embark upon an unpredictable, and probably protracted, War Against Terror, the work of first responders, which has always been dangerous, looks set to become even more so. All of us are now combatants in a war whose frontline runs through our city streets, our schools, our places of worship, our very homes. And in the forefront stand those men and women who have undertaken the protection of their communities and of America at large. Hence, the importance attached by the Department of Homeland Security to the work of the various law enforcement and rescue services and its determined efforts to lend them the fullest possible support.

Left: September 18, 2001, and police officers stand guard outside the New York Stock Exchange, although the city is determinedly, defiantly, "open for business." The huge flag in the background honors the dead, but Americans are already looking to a future in which peace and prosperity will prevail over destruction and terror.

HEROES OF THE HOUR

As she sat quietly in a Houston restaurant snatching a few minutes' break in a busy day, police officer Vanessa de la Garza almost fell out of her chair when a stranger walked up to offer her a torrent of congratulations. "I'm glad you're doing this job," said the stranger. "If no one else tells you today, let me be the one to say, 'Thank you for being a police officer.' " It was welcome praise, of course. Indeed, as Vanessa explained to the *Christian Science Monitor's* Abraham

Firefighters involved in rescue work head for home after a hard day's work among the rubble at Ground Zero: the tragedy revealed the astonishing reserves of courage and commitment to be found in apparently ordinary Americans.

New York Fire Department Battalion Chief Ralph Fago joins his fellow firefighters at an interfaith memorial service at Ground Zero. Rescue workers took a break from their labors to take part.

McLaughlin, she had been going through a "down" phase lately, wondering whether her work really made any difference, whether her career had any value.

The days and weeks following the cataclysm of September 11, 2001, were first and foremost a time of tragedy for first responders, as they mourned lost friends and realized that could have happened to them. Yet it was also a time when the glamorous Manhattan hostess simply had to have a firefighter or two on the guest list for her party and police officers were given standing ovations as they walked on patrol past outside cafes. And the positive reaction spread far and wide throughout the United States, coming down many hundreds of miles away from Lower Manhattan. Sergeant Horace Nero of the Saint Petersburg, Florida, Police Department, was flabbergasted to find kids coming up to him on the street and begging for his autograph.

But despite the praise, America's 436,000 police officers and 186,000 sheriffs' officers have their feet firmly on the ground. No one could be more conscious of the mounting dangers or increased workload they have brought. Officers appreciate the new respect they are shown by members of the public, who might previously have looked straight through them, but if the situation has its satisfactions, it has also undoubtedly brought more stress.

Part of the challenge is that they are now on the lookout for an entirely uncertain and unspecified threat. Matthew Webb, of the Saint Paul Police Department, told Minnesota Public Radio:

"I can remember being assigned to actually be part of a detail where we watched one of our patrol houses and I remember asking my supervisor, 'What do you want me to watch for?' And he said, 'Well, I don't know!'"

Police have consistently urged members of the public to be vigilant, but that has inevitably meant a few false alarms when people call in with concerns they previously would not have dreamt of

Right: A uniformed police officer helps his detective comrade to safety after the collapse of the World Trade Center, September 11, 2001—the choking dust enveloped everything for blocks around.

Passengers at the National Airport, Virginia, wait patiently in line at check-in. Delays we would have once felt were intolerable are now accepted as the price we have to pay for improved security.

reporting. "Somebody sees somebody on top of a building and the building is closed, they call the police now, whereas before they would automatically think it's the maintenance person," says Webb. Outside Saint Paul in Stillwater, Washington County, Deputy Sheriff Terry Hyde has noticed the difference, too. Job satisfaction is up, but so, too, are the challenges of what could formerly be a quiet routine. "Instead of just driving by and seeing the power plant," he

A NATION ON THE WATCH

Now with the Center for Defense Information in Washington, D.C., retired U.S. Army Colonel Daniel Smith summed up the thinking of many experts when he told the *Christian Science Monitor* that ordinary Americans needed to "shed their daily self-absorption and become more aware of their surroundings." In an age when many people, even school students, carry cellular phones wherever they go, we could all play a vital role as "eyes and ears" of the authorities. Abandoned cars, suspicious packages—indeed "anything that seems out of place," says Smith, should be promptly reported. "It may not seem much, but it can make all the difference."

A new philosophy? Well, not exactly. These are the principles on which Neighborhood Watch has worked for over 30 years. Effectively relaunched on the back of the current concern for Homeland Security, this nationwide program of public vigilance enables every man, woman, and child to make a contribution to the defense of the nation.

says, "instead of just driving by and not paying attention to it, we take a look. We turn and make it a point to look and make sure there's nothing going on." Here, too, there may be a fine line between praiseworthy public vigilance and irrational anxiety. One man was erroneously convinced he had fallen victim to a bioterrorist attack when he found a finger numb, and became convinced he had been contaminated by contact with a $10 bill in the change

A fire engine stands against the dramatic backdrop of the rubble mountain at Ground Zero: many firecrew were buried when the twin towers came crashing down.

from his groceries. Yet a high level of alertness is necessary if real outrages are to be prevented—better a few unfounded scares than a repeat of the tragedies of September 11.

KEEPING FAITH

Yet if first responders, such as police officers, firefighters, and paramedics, have enjoyed adulation as the "heroes of the hour," many have wondered what will happen in the longer term. As the Senate Select Committee on Intelligence was emphasizing, even in the immediate aftermath of September 11, terrorism should not be reacted to in haste. We must not arm ourselves for a one-time

A DIFFERENT OUTLOOK

Battalion Chief John Norman, placed in charge of the New York City Fire Department's Special Operations section, admits that progress in preparing and protecting firefighters for terrorist emergencies has been too slow. For years, before the events of September 11, 2001, there were warnings of the risk of terrorist attack, but the danger never seemed quite immediate enough and nothing was ever done. That is likely to change now, however, he told reporters from the *New York Times Herald-Record*: "September 11 woke a lot of people up." Money matters, he admits. Terrorists today can draw on huge resources; firefighters need the best of training and equipment if they are to stand in the frontline against them. Yet attitude may be just as important, he insists: "Awareness is the key. Treat everything as if it's the one that's going to kill you.... I think it's going to be harder to surprise us now."

"crisis," but take up weapons systematically against a "condition" that is likely to be with us for the foreseeable future.

John M. Buckman III, Fire Chief in Evansville, Indiana, and U.S. president of the International Association of Fire Chiefs, was grimly realistic when he spoke to *National Fire and Rescue Magazine* in 2002. "We all have short attention spans," he said. "The fire service—because of the loss of 343 lives—has the 'front page' today, so to speak. As time passes, we will be pushed off the front page."

The United States has over a million firefighters, of whom around 750,000 are volunteers. Buckman called for an additional

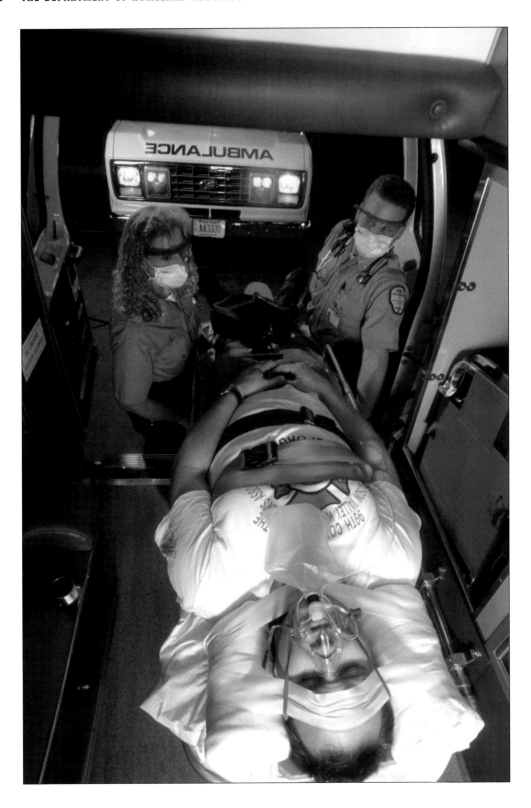

75,000 full-time professionals to be taken on and trained. He also insisted on the need for enhanced equipment and training for existing officers, who might now find themselves having to tackle dangers they never envisaged—notably, chemical and biological weapons. This issue caused controversy in New York City, where, by the beginning of 2002, grief was giving way to anger as firefighters asked whether the eloquent tributes they had received were going to be matched by substantive support. This would have to range from protection against chemical and biological toxins to more effective radios; from better flashlights to special "crisis routes," which would let fire engines speed to the scene of an incident through the grid-locked city. Such measures, say spokesmen, are necessary not only to save the lives of firefighters, but also to provide the best possible protection for members of the general public.

Already, plans are in the works for 50 teams to be trained to respond to incidents involving hazardous materials and to lend support in dealing with a range of other emergencies, from building collapses to marine rescues. Others are given more general training in aspects of antiterrorist work.

THE MEDICAL SERVICES

Doctors never saw themselves as soldiers before, but in the present situation, they, too, may have to come to the defense of their home-

Left: EMTs (Emergency Medical Technicians) place a patient in an ambulance before rushing him to the hospital: first responders now find themselves in the frontline in the war against terrorism.

ALL IN A DAY'S WORK?

"No matter what happens to you in your life, things can become routine," said Lieutenant Sherman Lacey of the U.S. Coast Guard in conversation with Adam Rogers of *Newsweek* magazine. "I really doubt anyone is treating this as routine." At the time of the New York attacks, the Coast Guard vessel the *Tahoma* had been patrolling the New England fisheries. Now it lies in New York Harbor looking to catch terrorists. Lacey will never forget the acrid smell of smoke from the scene of destruction. She and the rest of the crew had been aware of it from a distance of over 20 miles (32 km), long before they came in sight of that famous skyline minus its World Trade Center. Every ship that arrives in New York City is now checked thoroughly by the Coast Guard, and it looks as if they are going to be there for some time yet.

land. There are 155,000 EMTs (Emergency Medical Technicians) in the United States, and another terrorist attack may bring them to the frontline, along with other health care workers. Indeed, they will be essential in the case of a **covert** bioterrorist attack.

The alert nurse who puts two and two together and realizes that an apparently mundane miscellany of aches, pains, and sniffles adds up to something more sinister, may quite easily end up saving

Right: A Coast Guard vessel keeps guard in New York Harbor in the days after the September 11, 2001, attacks. Smoke rises skyward from the ruins of the World Trade Center in the background.

hundreds—perhaps even thousands—of lives. "The ER nurse must maintain a high level of suspicion all the time," says Jim Fenn of the Toledo Hospital, Ohio. "She must not be afraid to suggest to the physician some differential diagnoses that could indicate a biological attack, so at least they could rule that out." Again, the need is for vigilance—and better a false alarm than that a real attack be missed; sometimes the junior nurse might see something a senior doctor is too hurried or harassed to notice.

Some experts believe that our hospitals are our weakest point. Kim Jones is a registered nurse and is actively engaged in training hospital staff, police officers, and firefighters to work together in

A Coast Guard patrol boat, armed with machine guns, cruises around Boston Harbor, its crew on the lookout for the slightest sign of anything threatening.

America has always had to guard its frontiers: illegal immigration destabilizes our economy, while drug smuggling takes an appalling toll in our towns and cities. Here, officers of the Douglas, Arizona, Border Patrol check a party of undocumented aliens.

response to large-scale incidents. She told *Nurseweek* of her concerns that this sort of training had been neglected for far too long. In theory, hospitals are required to make provision for such emergencies, preparing incident plans and holding practice drills every six months. In practice, Jones remarked ruefully, too many managers have felt they had more important things to do. "Prior to September 11, most hospital administrators saw the disaster committee as just another annoying activity." Resources were—as ever—a problem.

Who wanted to invest in expensive decontamination facilities for attacks that would surely never happen? The money could be better spent on other equipment. With pressure to reduce costs, administrators never seemed to think it was a good time to stock up on

All Americans rallied around the flag after September 11, 2001, the United States united at once in grief and in firmness of resolve. These National Guardswomen helped provide security at Ground Zero as a part of the search-and-rescue operation.

antibiotics that, in all probability, would never be used. The attacks of September 11 jolted everyone out of their complacency, from the federal government downward. Five billion dollars in grants for hospital preparedness programs has now been proposed. Many local health authorities, like that of Los Angeles County, have undertaken searching reviews of plans, procedures, equipment, and readiness levels, and are acting energetically to bring hospitals and health care workers up to speed.

COOPERATION IS KEY

Off Savannah, Georgia, the Coast Guard stepped up its coastal patrols in the hours after the attacks of September 11, and it plans to maintain this level of vigilance until further notice. Charged with seeing to the protection of ports and harbors from South Carolina's Edisto River to the Florida border, the Coast Guard has been boarding all commercial vessels, screening crews, and checking cargoes. But officers are fully aware that they are unlikely to stumble upon a wanted terrorist or a stash of weaponry themselves; their role is to help in a collective effort to put the pieces of the puzzle into a larger picture.

"Coordination is very, very important," Commander James McDonald of the Coast Guard told the *Savannah Morning News*. His officials are in constant touch with colleagues in the FBI, the Customs Service, the Immigration and Naturalization Service, the Georgia Ports Authority police, and the Savannah Police Department—to name but a few. But cooperation cannot end with officials; it must include the public, too, if it is to be genuinely effective. Bucky Burnsed, of the Savannah Police Department, is quick to remind us: "It's incumbent upon all of us not to sit back. We're doing our jobs and we're going beyond what we have in the past. It's time for us to take more responsibility."

MINUTEMEN AND MINUTEWOMEN

Ron Wakeham, Fire Chief in Des Moines, Iowa, laughs wryly as he compares the current buzz with that surrounding the "Minutemen" of the Revolutionary War—ready at a minute's notice to go off and fight the British. He could take on 18 new firefighters in 2002, he told the *Christian Science Monitor*, and he expected over 600 applicants for the positions. Since September 11, 2001, we have been forced to rethink what heroism means and consider the many different ways in which American men and women might defend their country. Teachers coaching their classes in preparedness, veterinarians spotting the signs of what might be the deliberate infection of livestock herds, alert bus drivers, suspicious shop-keepers—all might find themselves in the position of being "first responders." The need for all of us to make a contribution to the nation's defense is only underlined by recent indications that the National Guard (the direct successors of the Minutemen) may have been taking on too much.

Many of those who are public-spirited enough to volunteer as Guardsmen and -women are already serving as police and prison officers, firefighters, and EMTs. As a result, their mobilization has sometimes had the effect of jeopardizing the strength of those agencies in which they normally work. These are early days, of course,

Only a couple of years ago, he would have seemed shockingly out of place; now this armed National Guardsman at Baltimore-Washington International Airport is an everyday presence.

and there is no doubt that such difficulties will be ironed out. Already, for instance, the new Transportation Security Administration has taken over the task of ensuring airport security. Having stepped into the breach at a crucial time while the new agency's officers were being recruited and trained, the National Guard can now turn its attentions to other areas, such as offering assistance to the Border Patrol. There is no doubting the competence, commitment, or courage of those already taking on the defense of our country—but the need is clear for all Americans to play their part.

BEHIND THE SCENES

"Think! Plan! Act!" urges John M. Buckman III, Fire Chief in Evansville, Indiana. The first two words of his slogan are every bit as crucial as the third. No one understands better the need for courage in action, but it must, he says, take place in the context of long-term thinking and careful planning.

America's first responders are entitled to every bit of praise that has been heaped upon them in recent months. Yet we should avoid romanticizing action at the expense of assiduous intelligence gathering and organization. In any case, no amount of physical courage will protect our financial markets against a terrorist-inspired computer crash; nor will gung-ho heroics prevent hackers from contriving a large-scale shutdown in our power supplies. America's intelligence agencies will have to work hand-in-hand with law enforcement and rescue services to ensure total readiness against any threat. It is up to the Department of Homeland Security to make sure all these organizations are pulling together. "We must open lines of communication and support like never before," said Tom Ridge on his swearing in as the Department's director. "The only turf we should be worried about protecting is the turf we stand on."

Left: Here, an airman banks his F-15D Eagle in the course of a training flight over the Pacific Ocean: all of America's armed services have been maintaining the maximum level of preparedness following the attacks on September 11, 2001.

FROM INFORMATION TO ACTION

In **liaison** with the intelligence services of our allies, the Central Intelligence Agency (CIA) has a role in gathering information about our terrorist enemies. Other agencies—from state and city police departments to the Border Patrol—also have their part to play in the task of intelligence gathering, but the job of interpreting such information falls upon the specialist services. The ultimate object of such investigations is, of course, to anticipate the actions of these groups and prevent them if possible.

Covert counterterrorist operations will be mounted against targets of this kind in order to preempt attack. By its very nature, these operations will remain shadowy , about which we shall hear little. What will remain important is "HUMINT," or human intelligence—information gathered by individual agents using the cloak-and-dagger methods of conventional espionage. Just as important is "SIGINT," or signals information, especially in an age when we can intercept Internet intelligence and e-mails.

A new Intelligence Awareness Office (IAO) has been established, headed by former National Security Advisor Admiral John M. Poindexter. It is equipped to identify terrorist communications along domestic telephone and e-mail networks. A kindred

Traders on the New York Stock Exchange shift huge sums of money at the click of a mouse: a major computer crash could cause untold economic devastation. Information technology is the engine of American life today, a tempting target for a new generation of "cyberterrorists."

President Bush meets Director George Tenet at the CIA's Virginia headquarters: the agency will play a vital role in ensuring homeland security in the coming years. Tenet is fully attuned to the threat— indeed, he had been warning of the dangers of international terrorism long before the fateful attacks of September 11, 2001.

Intelligence Exploitation Office (IEO) gathers comparable information from foreign sources so that terrorist conspiracies can be detected and prevented at an early stage.

Such ventures are taking us into uncharted waters, from both a legal and an ethical point of view. As Tom Ridge points out, they raise "cutting-edge questions of both privacy and civil liberties." He is only too mindful of the paradoxical problem that, in attempting to defend American democracy, we may risk endangering those very freedoms our democracy gives us. But in any free society, there has to be a trade-off between the unlimited rights of individuals to do as they like without fear of governmental interference, and the welfare and safety of that society at large.

Police officers at Hancock International Airport, Syracuse, New York, study security monitors. Thanks to modern surveillance systems, extensive complexes can be kept under the closest observation every minute of the day.

A SCALE OF READINESS

Announced by Tom Ridge in March 2002, the Homeland Security Advisory System (HSAS) identifies five different color-coded levels of threat and suggests protective measures:

- Green (low condition): little risk of terrorist attack; normal training routines and protective procedures are believed to be adequate
- Blue (guarded condition): general risk of terrorist attack; emergency response and command communications and basic procedures should be reviewed and rehearsed
- Yellow (elevated condition): significant risk of terrorist attack; surveillance should be stepped up in critical locations and emergency plans coordinated between different agencies
- Orange (high condition): high risk of terrorist attack; armed forces and law enforcement agencies are prepared; special precautions are taken at public events; and preparations are made for key personnel to be moved to alternate sites; access to high-security areas restricted to essential personnel only.
- Red (severe condition): severe risk of terrorist attack; public and government facilities to be closed; traffic and transportation to be halted or redirected; and emergency response personnel to be deployed.

Left: An F-117A "Stealth" Fighter slips across the sky, all but undetectable by enemy radar—but Americans will need all their vigilance to foil the threat posed by lower-tech terrorist infiltrators.

THE WAR AGAINST CYBERTERRORISM

In his speech of October 9, 2001, Homeland Security boss Tom Ridge spelled out the significance of information technology in modern American life—and the vital importance of its being protected against sabotage:

"Information technology pervades all aspects of our daily lives, of our national lives. Its presence is felt almost every moment of every day, by every American. It pervades everything from a shipment of goods, to communications, to emergency services, and the delivery of water and electricity to our homes. All of these aspects of our [lives] depend on a complex network of critical infrastructure information systems. Protecting this infrastructure is critically important.

"Disrupt, destroy, or shut down these information systems, and you shut down America as we know it and as we live it and as we experience it every day. We need to prevent disruptions; and when they occur, we need to make sure they are infrequent, short, and manageable. This is an enormously difficult challenge, because we must always remain one step ahead of the hackers."

IT AT RISK

It is possible that tomorrow's terrorist attack will be carried out invisibly. American inventors and technicians have led the world in developing information technology (IT), finding ways of using computers to organize just about every imaginable aspect of our lives. From water supply and sewage treatment to electricity distri-

Computer programmers in England wrestle with the problem posed by the ironically named "I love you" e-mail virus, which infected computer systems around the world in the spring of 2000.

bution and street lighting; from telecommunications to traffic lights; from airplane navigation systems to food preparation—all are now managed for us by advanced computer systems. There is hardly any area of life on which information technology does not impinge. The benefits are incalculable. So, too, however, are the potential risks. Are we putting too many of our eggs in the IT basket? The

A teenager surfs the Net—or is he running riot in some top-secret military system? Our reliance on IT is a source both of strength and vulnerability. In the "Information Age," knowledge is power, but that knowledge cannot easily be restricted, leaving us open to threats not only from criminals, but also from "cyberterrorists" and "hackers."

more complete our dependency, the greater our vulnerability.

There have already been several scares, from the mischievous exploits of high school hackers to the more damaging introduction of corrosive viruses that invade information systems and impede or destroy them. Then there are the organized criminal groups using such technology for the purposes of committing fraud or theft on an enormous scale. Finally, of course, there is the threat of sabotage by terrorists. Potentially, at least, such groups could wreak untold havoc in our society, creating meltdown in our financial system and bringing our economy to its knees. Moreover, government and social administration have come to depend strongly on such technologies. Computer systems hold everything from police and prison records to social security data.

In practice, of course, it would be both an extraordinarily resourceful—and extremely lucky—terrorist who succeeded in creating cyber-mayhem on such a massive scale. Our systems have their own defenses, which are continuously in the process of being refined. With the stakes so staggeringly high, however, it would be unwise for us to be complacent. Even an apparently minor software hitch could cause disruption, even disaster.

There are also ethical issues involved. A compromise must be struck between the rights of individuals and companies and the interests of the wider society. Most of the infrastructure that keeps America working—transportation, telecommunications, energy supply, and industry—is privately owned, although any difficulties have the potential to affect us all. Government is going to have to forge a working partnership with the private sector.

This will mean respecting company requirements for commercial confidentiality and independence of action while making sure that the concerns of the public are at the forefront. This will not be the easiest of tasks for Tom Ridge and his office. There will inevitably be disagreements about priorities along the way. With a little give and take, however, it should not prove impossible. The attack on the World Trade Center was quite specifically an attack on corporate

America; our business leaders appreciate as well as anyone the unusual requirements of an extraordinary situation.

KEEP THE FAITH

The attacks of September 2001 tested America's courage—and found it strong and true. Increasingly, however, our longer-term resolve, our moral stamina, will come under question. The fight for homeland security will be costly, not only in financial terms. In many ways, it will mean an end to the easy-going way of life we have previously enjoyed: extra time in airport lines, additional ID required in offices or banks, intrusive questions from wary public officials. It may now take nothing more than an inconsiderately parked car or a misdirected package to trigger a full-scale security alert. We will have to get used to a certain level of disruption and frustration. Ninety-nine times out of 100, it will turn out to be a false alarm, and public patience is going to be tried to its very limits. What will make matters worse is that these frustrations will bring no immediately obvious benefit—for there is nothing striking or memorable about a terrorist outrage that does not happen. Paradoxically, the more successful the Department of Homeland Security is, the less it will have to show for its work.

Right: October 11, 2001, and a vast congregation assembles on the Pentagon River Parade Field, Washington, D.C., to commemorate the 184 victims of the terrorist attack on the Pentagon Building a month before. Occasions such as this revealed a firmness of purpose and determination not to be defeated.

Here, United States Air Force General Richard B. Myers, Chairman of the Joint Chiefs of Staff, updates reporters on progress made in the ongoing War Against Terrorism.

It is up to us as Americans to hold our nerve and keep the faith. There will undoubtedly be major benefits to us all, not only in the prevention of future terrorist attacks, but also because this is a chance for Americans to come together and build a better, stronger society. Already local law enforcement officers are reporting that heightened public vigilance has helped suppress levels of more routine crime; antiterrorist alertness has created conditions in which muggers, burglars, and auto thieves have felt constrained from action. There may be other benefits, too. Health care workers and hospitals geared up to respond swiftly and efficiently to the first signs of bioterrorist attack are likely to deal more effectively with naturally originating outbreaks of infectious disease. The establishment of a "smart border," open to vital commerce but sealed against illegal imports, will help protect our society not only from terrorist weapons, but also from illegal drugs. All in all, as President Bush put it, "Homeland security will make America not only stronger, but, in many ways, better."

A month after the September 11, 2001, attacks, U.S. armed forces took the war to the terrorists. Here an F/A-18C Hornet is launched from the aircraft carrier USS *Carl Vinson* in the Arabian Sea, its mission to strike at Al Qaeda camps and installations on the ground in Afghanistan.

GLOSSARY

Annexation: to incorporate a country or other territory within the domain of a state

Anti-Semitism: hostility toward or discrimination against Jews as a religious, ethnic, or racial group

Armory: a supply of arms for defense or attack

Arms: a means (as a weapon) of offense or defense

Assassinate: to murder by sudden or secret attack, usually for impersonal reasons

Bioterrorism: the use of biological weapons—cultivated bacteria or viruses designed to spread sickness—creating casualties and panic among the civilian population; or to cause economic damage by spreading diseases in livestock or crops

Cold War: the lengthy confrontation between Communist Eastern Europe (and China) and the democratic countries of the West, which dominated world politics through much of the second half of the 20th century

Communism: a system of government and economics in which a single authoritarian party controls state-owned means of production

Covert: secret

Cyberterrorism: a form of terrorism that seeks to cause disruption by interfering with computer networks

Fascism: a mass movement of the 1920s and '30s fundamentally antagonistic to democratic ideals, yet gave people the illusion of involvement in the nation's well-being

Grievance: a cause of distress felt to afford reason for complaint or resistance

Guerrilla: a person who engages in irregular warfare, especially as a member of an independent unit carrying out harassment and sabotage

Liaison: communication for establishing and maintaining mutual understanding and cooperation between two groups

Pandemic: occurring over a wide geographic area and affecting an exceptionally high proportion of the population

Rogue state: a country, such as Iraq or North Korea, that ignores the conventions and laws set by the international community; rogue states often pose a threat, either through direct military action or by harboring terrorists

CHRONOLOGY

1917: The Russian Revolution, involving the overthrow of the tyrannical government of the czars in favor of what would turn out to be the more oppressive government of the Communist leaders.

1926: Mussolini, a fascist dictator, comes to power in Italy.

1933: Adolf Hitler comes to power in Germany; over the next few years, his National Socialist, or Nazi, party establishes an iron grip over every section of government and society. .

1939: September 1, German forces invade Poland, initiating the European phase of World War II.

1941: December 7, Germany's Axis ally, Japan, mounts a surprise attack on the U.S. fleet lying in Pearl Harbor; the United States is brought into what is now genuinely a world war.

1945: World War II comes to an end and the Cold War between the free West and Communist Eastern Europe and China begins.

1948: The state of Israel is founded in the aftermath of Hitler's Holocaust, but the new nation finds itself threatened by its Arab neighbors.

1979: The Iranian Revolution overthrows the shah, and Muslim fanatics take control; this represents a decisive moment in the rise of Islamic fundamentalism.

1989: The Soviet Union collapses, exhausted by a 10-year war in Afghanistan, and drained by years of economic stagnation and administrative inefficiency.

1990: Forces of Iraqi dictator Saddam Hussein invade neighboring Kuwait; in the ensuing Gulf War (1991), the aggressors are expelled, but the U.S.-led alliance stops short of interfering in the affairs of a sovereign state to the extent of actually deposing its leader.

1995: March 20, members of Aum Shinri Kyo ("Supreme Truth") cult mount sarin nerve-gas attack on Tokyo subway; April 19, Oklahoma City bombing highlights threat posed by "patriots" for whom the federal government is an enemy of (white) America.

2001: September 11, Islamic fundamentalists—members of Al Qaeda—fly hijacked airliners into the twin towers of the World Trade Center, New York, and into the Pentagon, Washington, D.C.; a fourth jet crashes in Pennsylvania after passengers overpower the hijackers; October 8, the Office of Homeland Security is established by President George W. Bush.

2002: President Bush establishes the Citizen Corps to mobilize voluntary action for homeland security at the community level; the Border Security and Visa Entry Reform Act is passed to tighten controls on America's borders.

FURTHER INFORMATION

The National Citizens' Crime Prevention Campaign has responded specifically to the terrorist alert of recent times to produce a series of media advertisements aimed at heightening general awareness and alertness. Its slogan is "United for a Stronger America." In conjunction with the government, it has published a free booklet offering sensible advice. You can get a copy of the *United for a Stronger America: Citizens' Preparedness Guide* simply by calling the toll-free number: 1-800-WEPREVENT.

USEFUL WEB SITES

For the latest news and information on homeland security, see: www.whitehouse.gov/news/releases

For the Anser Institute for Homeland Security, see: www.homelanddefense.org/bulletin

Try this site if you would like to make a contribution toward the defense of the United States: www.citizencorps.gov

For the National Homeland Security Knowledgebase—the definitive site for homeland security information, see: www.twotigersonline.com/resources

FURTHER READING

Armstrong, Karen. *Islam: A Short History*. New York: Modern Library, 2000.

Hoge, James F., Jr., and Gideon Rose. *How Did This Happen? Terrorism and the New War*. New York: Public Affairs, 2001.

Daalder, Ivo H., I.M. Destler, Robert E. Litan, Michael E. O'Hanlon, and Peter Orszag. *Achieving Homeland Security*. Washington, D.C.: Brookings Institution, 2002.

ABOUT THE AUTHOR

Michael Kerrigan was born in Liverpool, England, and educated at St. Edward's College, from where he won an Open Scholarship to University College, Oxford. He lived for a time in the United States, spending time first at Princeton, followed by a period working in publishing in New York. Since then he has been a freelance writer and journalist, with commissions across a very wide range of subjects, but with a special interest in social policy and defense issues. Within this field, he has written on every region of the world. His work has been published by leading international educational publishers, including the BBC, Dorling Kindersley, Time-Life, and Reader's Digest Books. His work as a journalist includes regular contributions to the *Times Literary Supplement*, London, as well as a weekly column in the *Scotsman* newspaper, Edinburgh, where he now lives with his wife and their two small children.

INDEX

References in italics refer to illustrations